A New True Book

SPIDERS

By Illa Podendorf

*This "true book" was prepared
under the direction of
Illa Podendorf,
formerly with the Laboratory School,
University of Chicago*

 CHILDRENS PRESS, CHICAGO

Garden spider

PHOTO CREDITS

Lynn M. Stone—Cover, 2, 4 (bottom left), 7 (left) 9 (top), 13 (bottom), 16, 18 (2 photos), 20, 23, 28, 30, 32, 36 (bottom), 37, 38 (2 photos), 44 (bottom left and right)

James P. Rowan—4 (top left and bottom right), 7 (right), 9 (bottom), 10 (right), 13 (top), 15, 25 (2 photos), 42, 44 (middle right)

Allan Roberts—21, 26, 34, 44 (top)

Bill Thomas—36 (top)

Reinhard Brucker—4 (top right)

© Kjell B. Sandved, Smithsonian Institution—41

Judy Potzler—4 (middle right)

Milton Cole—10 (left)

COVER—Fishing spider

Library of Congress Cataloging in Publication Data

Podendorf, Illa.
  Spiders.

  (A New true book)
  Revised edition of: The true book of spiders. 1962.
  Summary: Introduces spiders and their
habits: where they live, what they eat, how
they move and protect themselves, how they
help and harm us, and why they are called
engineers.
  1. Spiders—Juvenile literature.   [Spiders]
I. Title.
QL458.4.P6   595.4'4   81-38444
ISBN 0-516-01653-9   AACR2

TABLE OF CONTENTS

WHAT ARE SPIDERS?

Each of these animals belongs to a different group. Can you tell which one is the spider?

You know that the bird, the fish, and the snake are not spiders. You know that the bee is an insect that flies. Then you know that the animal with the plump body and long legs must be a spider.

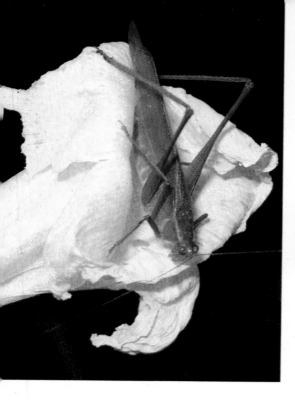

Above: Grass spider
Left: Katydid

Here are pictures of another spider and another insect. You know that the katydid is an insect. Can you see how spiders are different from insects?

Let's find out what
spiders have that makes
them different from insects.
Look carefully at these
different kinds of spiders.
How are they alike? How
many legs do they have?

Fishing spider

Funnel weaver spider

All spiders have eight legs.

Here are pictures of two different kinds of insects. Each insect has six legs. All insects have six legs.

Damsel fly

Dogbone leaf beetle

Spiders are different
from insects in another
way. All spider bodies are
in two parts—the head and
the abdomen. The
abdomen is the plump
part.

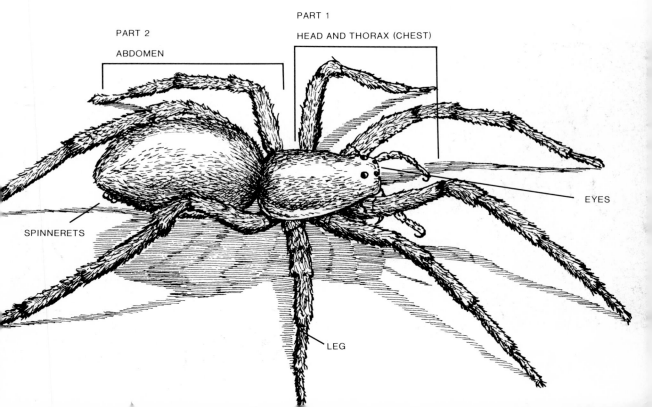

PART 2
ABDOMEN

PART 1
HEAD AND THORAX (CHEST)

EYES

SPINNERETS

LEG

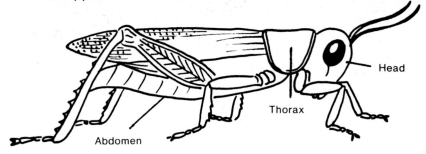

Grasshopper

Head

Thorax

Abdomen

All insect bodies are in three parts. The body part between the head and the abdomen is called the thorax. The legs of an insect are fastened to the thorax.

There is another difference between spiders and insects. Spiders do not have feelers. All insects have feelers.

Grasshopper

It is easy to see the six legs and the feelers on this insect.

How many legs does this spider have? Can you see any feelers?

Wolf spider

13

ARE ALL SPIDERS ALIKE?

All spiders have eight legs and plump bodies. They do not have feelers.

Each kind of spider has a name of its own.

Spiders are alike in some ways.

They are different from each other, too.

Some spiders are bigger than others.

Some spiders have fuzzy bodies and others do not.

Some spiders have longer legs than others.

Most spiders have eight eyes.

Nursery web spider

Spiders live in different
kinds of places.

Some live where it is hot.
Others live where it is cold.

Some live where it is
wet, and some live where
it is dry.

Some live in houses.

Some live in gardens.

Some spiders live in water. They come to the top of the water for air.

Bubbles of air collect on hairs of their legs. They take this air down and store it at the bottom of the water. When the air is gone, they come up for more air bubbles.

Some spiders live in the ground.

Spiders eat butterflies and grasshoppers.

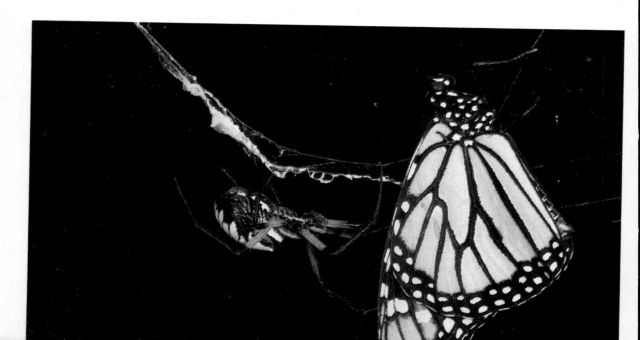

WHAT DO SPIDERS EAT?

Spiders eat other animals.

They eat many insects.

Big spiders can catch tadpoles and even birds.

Spiders eat only insects and other animals that they catch themselves. They do not eat food that other animals catch.

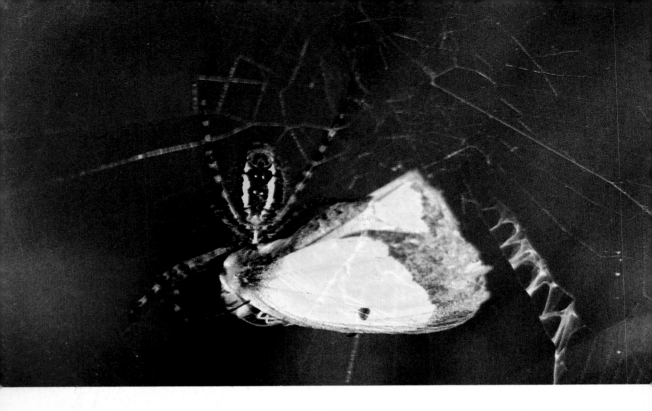

Many spiders catch food
in their webs.

A trap-door spider waits
for an insect to come
along and get caught in its
trap.

Wolf spider

   Some spiders hunt for
their food. The wolf spider
hunts insects. It goes after
an insect when it sees
one.

HOW DO SPIDERS MOVE FROM PLACE TO PLACE?

Spiders can run fast with their eight legs. They can run, walk, and jump.

You can guess how the jumping spider got its name.

Jumping spider landing on a leaf

Spiders travel in other ways, too. Some of them spin threads. When there are enough threads, they hang on and are blown through the air by the wind.

HOW DO SPIDERS PROTECT THEMSELVES?

Sometimes spiders run fast to get away from enemies.

When the enemies move fast, too, spiders must protect themselves in other ways.

Above: Mexican tarantula
Left: American tarantula

A tarantula spider may bite its enemy. Sometimes the enemy is paralyzed by the bite and then the spider has a chance to escape.

House spider with egg sac in web

Some kinds of spiders spin loose threads to trap their enemies.

Some kinds of mother spiders spin egg cases to protect eggs and young spiders. The outside of the egg cases makes it hard for enemies to harm young spiders or eggs.

Green lynx spider

The color of some spiders helps them to hide from their enemies. They are not easily seen.

Scientists call this protective coloration.

The house spider sometimes acts as though it is dead when an enemy comes near.

Sometimes an enemy gets caught in the web of a spider. The spider quickly spins a thread and slides down it. When the enemy is gone, the spider may climb up the thread to the web again.

A trap-door spider closes the door and holds it shut. The enemy cannot get it.

Two spiders may get into a fight. If a spider happens to get into a fight and lose a leg, a new leg will grow back in its place.

Spiders can grow new legs.

HOW ARE SPIDERS HELPFUL TO US?

Most kinds of spiders are helpful to us. They eat insects that are harmful to us. Some of the insects spiders eat carry disease. Flies and mosquitoes carry disease. Some other insects harm our plants. Locusts and grasshoppers eat plants we need.

This spider's bite is poisonous to insects.

HOW ARE SPIDERS HARMFUL TO US?

Sometimes spiders eat insects that are not our enemies. We like to have them eat the harmful ones, but not the helpful ones.

The bite of most spiders is poisonous to insects and small animals. But very few spiders can bite and hurt people.

Female black widow spider

The bite of the black widow spider is dangerous. It is very poisonous. It is easy to tell a black widow by its hour-glass marking. Only the female spider, which is bigger than the male, is known to bite.

The brown recluse spider and the sack spider have very poisonous bites, too.

Above: Basket web
Right: Close-up of
dew covered web

WHY ARE SPIDERS SOMETIMES CALLED ENGINEERS?

Spiders are famous for the kinds of webs that they can spin.

Some of the webs are like wheels. We call them orb webs. Garden spiders make orb webs.

A grass spider builds a funnel web.

A triangle spider builds a triangle web.

Some spiders make dome webs. Others make hammock webs.

Some spiders build bridges with their silk threads.

A spider uses the silk that it spins for many purposes.

It may make an egg case.

It may use silk threads for traveling.

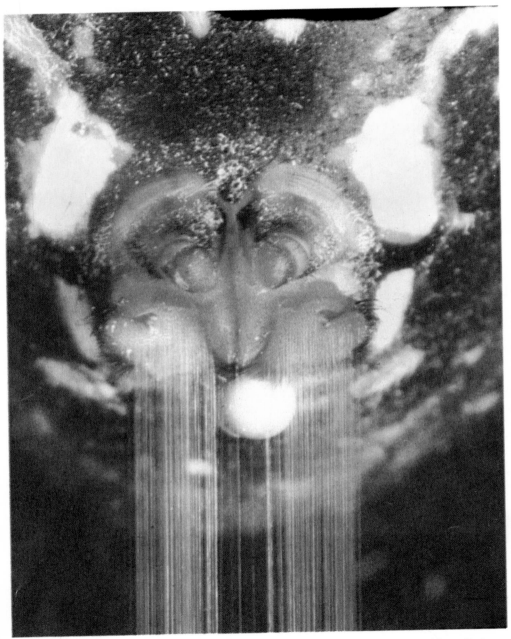

Silk spinning orb weaver spider from New Guinea

Golden garden spider

It may wrap up some of its food in the silk threads.

A spider may line its home with its silk.

It may make a food-catching web with silk thread.

This is why spiders are often called engineers.

Above: Cave spider
Right: Crab spider
Below Right: Baby spiders in nursery web
Below: Golden silk spider

There are thousands of different spiders. Some scientists think there may be more than 30,000 different kinds. Each kind has its own way of living.

Do not handle spiders.

Look for spiders in their natural homes and watch them. They are fun to watch.

WORDS YOU SHOULD KNOW

abdomen (ab • DOH • min) — the part of an insect's or spider's body that is at the end away from the head

black widow (BLACK WID • oh) — a spider that has a poisonous bite

brown recluse (BROWN REK • loose) — a spider that is brown and has a poisonous bite

dangerous (DAIN • jer • us) — full of harm or injury; risky

disease (dih • ZEEZE) — sickness; illness

dome (DOHME) — a rounded roof

enemy (EN • ih • mee) — not a friend

engineer (en • jin • EER) — a person who builds things

escape (es • KAIP) — to get free; break loose

famous (FAY • MUS) — well known

fasten (FASS • in) — attach

feeler (FEEL • er) — part of an insect's head that is used for finding out what is around

funnel web (FUN • ihl WEB) — a web in the shape of a cone

fuzzy (FUZ • ee) — covered with fine fur or hair

hammock web (HAM • uck WEB) — a web that hangs between two points

harm — injure; damage

hour-glass — two glass containers connected at the narrow parts

insect — an animal with six legs and three body parts

locust (LOW • kust) — a type of grasshopper

orb web — a web made in a round shape

plump — rounded and full

paralyze (PAIR • uh • lize) — to be unable to move

poison (POY • zun) — something that can cause injury, sickness, or death

protective coloration (pro • TEK • tiv kul • er • AY • shun) — to be the same color as the background so something cannot be seen

tadpole (TAD • pohl) — a frog or toad that has just hatched and lives underwater

tarantula (tah • RAN • choo • la) — a large, hairy spider

telescope (TELL • ess • cope) — an instrument that makes far-away objects look bigger and closer

thorax (THOR • ax) — the part of an insect's or spider's body right behind the head

triangle web (TRY • ang • il WEB) — a web that has three sides

web — a network of fine, silky threads woven by a spider

INDEX

About the author

Born and raised in western Iowa, Illa Podendorf has had experience teaching science at both elementary and high school levels. For many years she served as head of the Science Department, Laboratory School, University of Chicago and is currently consultant on the series of True Books and author of many of them. A pioneer in creative teaching, she has been especially successful in working with the gifted child.